RAYFISH

Rayfish

Mary Hickman

OMNIDAWN PUBLISHING

OAKLAND, CALIFORNIA

2017

Cover art by Robert Fernandez
Rayfish, mixed media, 2016

Cover and interior typefaces: Minion Pro

Interior design by Cassandra Smith

Offset printed in the United States
by Edwards Brothers Malloy, Ann Arbor, Michigan
On 55# Glatfelter B18 Antique
Acid Free Archival Quality Recycled Paper

Library of Congress Cataloging-in-Publication Data

Names: Hickman, Mary, 1979- author.
Title: Rayfish / Mary Hickman.
Description: Oakland, California : Omnidawn Publishing, 2017. | Includes
  bibliographical references.
Identifiers: LCCN 2016045481 | ISBN 9781632430311 (pbk. : alk. paper)
Classification: LCC PS3608.I2755 A6 2017 | DDC 811/.6--dc23
LC record available at https://lccn.loc.gov/2016045481

Published by Omnidawn Publishing, Oakland, California
www.omnidawn.com   (510) 237-5472   (800) 792-4957
10 9 8 7 6 5 4 3 2 1
ISBN: 978-1-63243-031-1

for Robert

I could say as much for what we call the "work of art." How do we recognize such a work? Only by the following: That faced with it, we do not stay faced, but we meet, we strike, we are struck, we lose our envelope just as this thing, this work, loses its own—its forms, its mannerisms. We develop within it as it does within us… We do not remain in ourselves, we do not leave ourselves. Just in between: we get a bump, a bruise, a blood clot. Being gets out of there swollen, tumescent, distended. Neither fluid such as water immanent to water, nor leaping such as a dolphin transcending waves. Rather dull, dingy and uncertain like a Medusa between two waters.

—Jean-Luc Nancy

I

Shenzhen

My brother insists that cracking melon seeds bears relation to speech.
The only content has been eaten. Shell empty, no content remains. Live
action then silence or, at the most, echo. We fill bottle after bottle with
husks. When we are on our own, carving our names into trunks in the
lychee grove, he cuts his hand. The knife slips, slicing his thumb and
forefinger. As blood covers his arm, my brother is firework and flag,
bright pain and strange happiness. How does one work with chaos as
a material for life? I can't predict how the sap of the tree and the blood
of the fist will behave! I perch on the branch, touch my heel, grasp
my right foot in my left hand, hold cold foot in warm palm and think
Now I know myself by heart. Now I know my heart, too. The palm
shows the measure of the trunk, the trunk the measure of the torso. I
distinguish the layers of my fingers; I feel areas of pain, plumes of pain.
Do you see these living figures? I ask. They are flashes of lightning
resembling ideas. They make me understand from there to here. On
our way to the hospital, we meet a woman sweeping the street. She
picks up a wrapper, spits on it, and presses it to his cut. When she was
a child, she says, buying flowers was very bourgeois, but she bought
tissue paper and brought it home to make roses. Ropes of bright red
firecrackers hang the length of the skyscrapers. Lit, they rip across eye

and ear with violence as the smell of gunpowder floats back. The real beauty of the Roman candle, the bottle rocket, or the fire-flower is they fan into new forms. Fingers become petals of paper and flame. All these symbols—paper, gunpowder, pine trees—I hold these elements in my hands and I ignite them to see what may be. In the hospital, he shakes with pain on the dingy sheets. I curl up at the foot of the bed. If I shift, the mattress exhales a scent like wet earth. I love this flow of sleep that comes down on me like snow as I play dead. I hold his foot to comfort him. His attention stops at the thin part of the world. Linen becomes sand and milk, becomes a caress on the skin of my brother who, by playing dead, becomes all child and enters a new experience of home. The resting child is encircled by the impersonal. To it, he owes his sudden firmness, perpetually destroying, perpetually rebuilding. Blood, too, is a tissue. "姐" he mutters. *Sister.* He sucks red ropes back into sleep.

Still Life with Rayfish

Soutine attempts to keep the color of his first carcasses fresh with buckets of blood. The neighbors hate the stench and the flies but he continues to pour blood over the bodies until he is ordered by the police to stop. Only then does he use formaldehyde. He isn't preserving the flesh, just refreshing it, maintaining the life-color of the carcass and painting that blood as lush. He is not emulating and there is no reminiscence. When Soutine's last privately owned carcass painting, *Le boeuf écorché*, was auctioned recently, the seller expected to get something like seven to eight million dollars. In the catalog description, Christie's lingers over Soutine's early intense poverty and the sudden relief of that poverty when he sold a large number of paintings to a banker. *Le boeuf écorché* represents a point at which Soutine could afford to buy whole beef sides just to look at rather than eat. *Le boeuf* sold for fourteen million dollars, which I find depressing. Or it misses the point. If anyone blends the line between still life and portrait, it's Soutine. The still life reflects portraiture without any deliberate reminiscence. Soutine's brothers beat him mercilessly. Their cruelty became a ritual. One day when Soutine was sixteen, he approached a pious Jew to ask him to pose for a portrait. The next day this man's son and his friends beat Soutine. It was a week before he walked again. Why is this story retold so often? I don't think I create heroes in my portraits in the conventional romantic or poetic sense. Soutine fights against the monsters. He fights against neuroticism and fear. His portrait can be made in many ways but always the same image. Sometimes, in fact, I make the same portrait. Say *Still Life with Rayfish*. It could have been a fairytale. My way of making a fable from the portrait is my way of telling it. I simply told it as I did. But our hero is really there: the one in the portrait who possesses the feel of his own life. This is part of Soutine's process also: to see the forbidden thing and paint it, to severely constrict his subject within the frame and enclose space. He imprisons the image within the image. In Chardin's *Rayfish*, the ray at rest has become a ghost already, nearly translucent at the mouth and eyes. In *Still Life with Rayfish*, Soutine attempts a portrait of Chardin. This ray rises howling from the table, its membranous belly shuddering. Its entrails glow with warmth. *Today you will eat dead things and make them into something living: but when you will be in light, what will you do then? For then you become two instead of one; and when you become two, what will you do then?* Do I mean that in all our portraits we tell the same story? But I can't say I have a special direction, although I feel a certain evolution in myself, in the ways I find of saying things. Let's call this a transition from attention to grace. When Soutine works in serial, painting the same object again and again, the paintings convulse. Seen side by side, their convulsions evoke sensation. I see great possibilities by shifting the wings, moving the feathers or necks. Swirling, lacerated flesh swells against blue or red or green backgrounds. The figure of the bird, whirling fowl of penitence, beats even as darker backdrops threaten to swallow it. *The body which depends upon a body is unfortunate, and the soul which depends upon these two is unfortunate.* In this first portrait of the rayfish, the ray is pulled up by its wings, each wing pierced with wire hung from the stone wall behind. Or the next ray hovers over the table, ascending; it swoops midair. Soutine presents the butchered animal opened, taken to pieces, bloody, glistening, shimmering yet conspicuously dead. I devour a skin that is grotesque with demonic aura, the terror and humor of its textures. I paint a skin made from sheer white curtains blowing at windows in stark sun. I make a figure from gray feathers stuck to my neck with sweat. I build whole visions of life out of the swirling black velvet of a woman's dress as she wades into water. That wet velvet billows, a second skin, sensual, dragging her under, pulling her out to sea. In *La Dolce Vita*, the soft, dark flesh of the monstrous ray is bound tightly by the fishermen's net as the ray is hauled onto the beach. "You will make a million with this fish!" "It's alive!" "It's been dead three days." Rolled onto its back, its mouth pulls open and one black eye stares back. Its slick surface resembles the protoplasmic source of all things. It insists on looking. The guardian angel of Adrian Lyne's *Jacob's Ladder* quotes Meister Eckhart to the dying Jacob: "Eckhart saw hell too. He said: 'the only thing that burns in hell is the part of you that won't let go of your life, your memories, your attachments. They burn them all away. But they're not punishing you,' he said. 'They're freeing your soul. . . . If you've made your peace, then the devils are really angels freeing you from the Earth.'" I picture the nets around the rayfish as sutures pulled from its flesh, releasing the wings to unfold. I imagine the scarred eyes of the surgeon's attendant in *Jacob's Ladder* as two layers of flesh folded over. Bones and lumps of flesh piled in the hallway, faces vacant or badly twisted: Lyne's "body horror technique." The face moves with an alien speed, a filmic sensation of seizure, fit, possession, mutation. *He who has known the world has fallen into the body, and he that has fallen into the body, the world is not worthy of him.* The ray's blank eye and the attending angel's carved sockets equally terrify. Soutine's eddies in oil capture the ray's flesh. He structures my seeing; he imparts vision. I pamper this slight ghost—I encourage it. It takes shape slowly. It takes possession. "Once I saw the village butcher slice the neck of a bird and drain the blood out of it. I wanted to cry out, but his joyful expression caught the sound in my throat." Soutine pats his throat and continues, "This cry, I always feel it there. When, as a child, I drew a crude portrait of my professor, I tried to rid myself of this cry, but in vain. When I painted the beef carcass it was still this cry that I wanted to liberate. I have still not succeeded."

ANDY WARHOL

Andy only wants to be told about his body by others. Like if I am
on the phone with him, standing here completely naked, looking at
my stretch marks. If, right now, I am looking at the scar on my side
from my abscessed breastbone and I am looking at the scar on my
leg from where I fell in the garden, he asks, "What about *my* scars?
What are they proof of?" Andy is all eye—air and desert. Or he is
inward illumination. This silence of flesh, if it is the essence of Andy,
is also the image we make from his scars, his blisters, craters, pocks,
and scabs. Often we arrive at the point at which the Andy I offer the
viewer, and offer back to Andy, creases or buckles. It curls in humidity,
becomes rigid, vulnerable, loses flexibility. It's not that I can't imagine
Andy's abdomen alongside my own scarred chest, but I remember
reading how embarrassed he was in the hospital. He started to collect
things. The nuns encouraged him to collect stamps. Coins, too. He
never wants to bring his personal life into his work in a direct way. It
should never be read as, "I'm telling you about my personal life, my
friends, this is what's happened." I'd never go to Andy to understand
flesh, to think about these bodies, but if I wanted to know, say, about
quilts, about whether or not this is a real American quilt or if this
Christmas was a real American Christmas, a magazine Christmas,

I'd ask Andy. Ask, are these Levis, not just bluejeans? And of course he'd know. "I want to die with my bluejeans on," and all that. The stitching involved in my portrait of Andy, in order to distance the needle, to capture what we feel as we notice the expression he wears in the Avedon photo when he lifts his shirt for us...Well, embroidery is not painting, even if it seems to be. And to sew flesh, to work in a field that teaches you to close wounds, is to work without emotion, shadowy. Andy does not posses a dynamic glance but one that is fixed, immobile, myopic in the rigidity of its stitching. He had a nightmare. He was taken to a clinic. He dreamed of a charity to cheer up people who were horribly disfigured, people who had to wear plastic across their faces and underneath: nothing. We had this nightmare together or it was his nightmare alone but he repeated it so often it is now nearly my memory. "When the alcohol is dry," he says, "I am ready to apply the flesh-colored paint that doesn't resemble any human flesh I've ever seen, though it does come pretty close to mine." As a child I visited the Great Wall. As a child I rode trains through the Gobi desert. As a child I wanted nothing more than bluejeans. I saw the yellow crust of the Gobi, the olive uniforms of the guards, each stone of the wall the size of my leg and the steps in places impassable. What I realize, what the image of Andy reveals to Andy, is that his scars do not describe engrossing stories, do not stimulate indecent cravings. The same figures repeat in bands, stitched with the tails gathered in knots, drawn in bundles, obscuring the chest or connecting it in lines of communication. When Andy looks in the mirror, when he is nothing and with no sense of existence, I am sure I'm going to look in the mirror and see nothing. People are always calling Andy a mirror and if a mirror looks into a mirror what is there to see? When the sun extracts the last drop of moisture from the skin, the skin shrinks and forms intricate patterns. When the heat cracks the chest, it draws salt, covering the chest in a fine web of seams. This is what we call a contemporary landscape. *Still Life and Desire.* You were just lying there and I was standing over you crying. You kept telling me not to make you laugh, it really hurt. "And…? And…?" he asks. He will not stop asking. If someone else talks about it, I listen, I hear the words, and I think maybe it's all true. What about *your* scars, I say. I'll tell you about *your* scars. You put them to work for you. They're the best thing you have. These bodies, this molten mass of bodies constantly seething and circulating, form cracks in the dark, cooled skin over the glowing image of Andy. This enables me to be happy with this piece, to sweeten the figure of Andy, to allow him to remain as he insists upon remaining: suspended in a vaporous narrative. We dissolve desire to enter the heart of Andy. There are bones in the Great Wall. My finger finds a finger-bone. There are wrists in this wall. And a pelvis, a pelvis is a fossil.

II

I Have Had Many Near-Death Experiences

Watching Kazuo Ohno dancing *Mother*, I end up thinking, *Oh mama mama, my turtledove*. Only fairytales come to mind. The song in "The Juniper Tree" sung by the murdered son become a bird: "My mother she killed me / My father he ate me / My sister Marlene gathered my bones / Tied them in a scarf / Laid them beneath the juniper tree." In *Mother*, when the music stops, the spotlight widens to reveal an audience perfectly stilled. It sounds as if Kazuo calls up North Sea winds from every direction, calls up a landscape of ragged cliffs and swells. Kazuo's rawness must be the rawness of the sea. He renders each pulsating twisting move of jellyfish in dance. How human bodies become. He has seen thousands of jellies circling, victims of hunger or disease, soldiers buried at sea, men he knew in the war. He was a prisoner of war. Tuesday was yesterday, but today is Wednesday. They confirmed Wednesday that he died on Tuesday. Is Tuesday in Japan Wednesday here? In *Mother*, the gestures are not eroticism, not desire but percussive violence. He stamps ankles into strength. The dance demands he unlearn his upright body, unlock shoulder from spine, disarticulate each confined, trained joint. In Butoh, bodies distort beyond etiquette and beyond beauty, becoming crippled ships, bent forest floor. He must unfold his body, loosen the face and prepare for a face made utterly unfamiliar. Tracking his own corpse, he finds a face so fixed even agony cannot be found there. He dances the sharp chirping of insects, the animal's lowing, and thus unmoors his body. People say many things about Kazuo's body: It is a corpse standing, an outcry from somewhere outside the culture of flesh. I find working from life so intimidating—I find it hard to do. I have had many near-death experiences, moments when I certainly might have died. On a mountain road near Taiwan's north coast, I bent over a cliff edge to pick flowers and fell thirty feet. When I looked up, my companion gestured for me to stay still. He was yelling *Don't move!* I moved and felt myself drop six inches. Only branches supported me and, below, the cliff roped in mist. As Kazuo builds a dance, it's like adding layers of flesh. I hesitate to create a myth about Kazuo since we have to continue his endeavors. He needed a recipient. We have to be receptive. There is a moment when the image starts to breathe. There is something unsettled about the image, like form passing into a gesture that is *live.* Eight ghostly-white bodies emerge from the sea and scramble over the rocks. They move sideways over the sharp rocks. They unfurl long red ribbons from their mouths, something that words can't touch. Exploring caves underwater, squeezing through smaller and smaller openings but always sure there would be another opening ahead, I was diving without equipment. I saw the reef and a school of squid just beyond. When my lungful of air began to run out,

I tried to surface, and I saw a hole in the rock leading up. As I swam, the opening narrowed. I had no air left to go back the way I'd come or look for another way, but I couldn't get through. I thought I'd pass out and drown. I forced myself to push my body upward and shoved my body through the tube of rock until I was scraped and bleeding but breaking the surface. I dragged my body to the surface.

If the Heart Does Not Restart

As I try to wonder about a stroke, an embolism, a rupture, or pancreatic pathologies, sudden invasive virulence, instead I think, *Go to the store for Roundup*. Then the French neighbor gardening in her silk blouse hints chemicals might take care of the grasses on our side, the ones choking the basil. But I say bittersweet or Japanese creeper on the fence, what's the difference. She's saying it again. "Sweet Autumn clematis should be more vigorous than the large-flowered clematis hybrids." And on the internet: "I know she fought with every ounce of strength." Or, "She died peacefully at home." An appropriate response to this: bullshit. She wrote so many books. She is writing so many books. All of these books undulate from her like swells, like the yellow liquid left in the tube after selling platelets. I'm not saying vampiric when I think of everything going wrong in the blood. Or the tubes carrying blood. Or blood keeps going where it shouldn't in quantities the brain can't handle. When he took a job counseling terminal patients, when he no longer had clients but patients, then he had the stroke. He stroked. Who knows how to respond to this? During surgeries, I watched the blood spinning through tubes, getting aerated, oxygenated, whipped up and sent back to the limbs. I wished there was less hard blue plastic, less crisscrossing of tubes and wires. My nightmares in recent years involve violating the sterile field. I touch my neck, then I touch the edge of the wound, and I am filled with shame but also fear because maybe now there's nothing to be done since I've contaminated the chest cavity and the patient will most likely move on to infection, fever, death, but I won't know because, one, I'll wake up or, two, *wakes up* will stop mattering. Option three involves me trying to cry in the locker room bathroom but instead wanting a sandwich, not knowing the patient's *name* anyway. I'm on the hunt here, following the vine to its root only to find it's one vine among twelve and we'd better get the shovel or decide this is just wisteria that hasn't bloomed yet. In a nightmare, I once vomited on a patient. I just missed the chest cavity. Awake, I really did drop many valuable things. One of the things given to me to hold was the heart itself. I never held a warm heart but sometimes wish I had. I think I would have cried more for a warm heart that refused to restart. The cold ones, nesting in sterile ice, never inspired much hope of life. The real difference between a surgery that ends well and one that doesn't is the way the body is closed. If the surgery is successful, then the patient's heart restarts and the pressure comes up. A regular rhythm is achieved, and we close each layer— heart, sternum, any little blood vessels, fat, each layer of dermis. If the heart does not restart, there is no careful sewing. A staple gun closes the skin but not the layers underneath. The sternum is still pulled closed with wires but fewer and less neatly tied. I grab the incision's edges, tug them together with one hand, and with the other start the grating plastic *click click click* of the gun. The table is pulled away and the drapes peeled off the skin. We wipe away the blood and the betadine. We pull the blanket to the chin. I never stick around to see what happens next. Or I do and now I don't know.

III

TOTAL HIP REPLACEMENT

I lived with her for months to learn the steps. Her building, near what was once the heart of Catalan power, has been converted, mutilated, and restored many times since Roman rule. It was late March, the rainy season. I knew that this was the right time for me to be there. I began, and simultaneously she began to have trouble with her hip. She had invited me to make paper, which is a watery process and requires space. The studio fills with water and you feel the possibility to make something bright white, atmospheric. Part of me would like to make work that's minimal, well organized, clean, quiet and comprehensible. But hands learn to do things. They have to learn to read. If you miss this step, you can slip alignment. If you do not read, if you find you're only lying on your back, staring at the ceiling, what kind of work happens? White Dada at its most obscene. The minute I set my eyes on an animal, I know what it is. Francis Bacon's suit sleeks the gray of sitting room walls. Lucian Freud pulls a zebra head against the stripes on his chest. Andy Warhol's talc hands fold talc hands. *Nothing changes from generation to generation except the thing seen and that makes a composition.* In this one, "It's light, it's dark," she laughs. Women did not feel like mine. I have immense conviction while making this work. The images I love best of all exemplify Dada. The world will not repeat it. You see, I'm not interested in paper as a portrait or in portraits as such. I don't use the anatomy of my face because I like it. No. I use it because it pulls something from *inside*. A neurosis. Making paper, the screen must be perfect, not warped but perfectly smooth. The water needs to flow down the screen in the right patterns across the pulp. In the same way, when you see a surgeon covered head-to-toe in a white paper jumpsuit, when you see only his eyes through the window of the hood and the window is striped with irrigation fluid, you begin to understand something about time. In the operating room, she's lying on her side, hip pocket exposed, and there's water on the floor. The surgeon keeps the water flowing to wet the bone dust rising from the only visible flesh. I bring a cup sewn from rags. She arrives in a self sewn from pulp. Saw touches bone. Her cup fills. We begin to speak. We expel ourselves. I don't find this tragic. The woman on the beach wears a glass eye, a solar flare shaped like a horn. And farther out to sea, whipped whites, lilac-tainted whites woven into waves on white screen, cut from this single white page.

Everything Is Autobiography and Everything Is a Portrait

Your body in motion calls me to look. You know just how to move. You are determined to move just so. If I could make my image of you *do* anything, what could I imagine myself becoming? Rather than painting on canvas or sculpting in clay, I am driven to put all these ideas on myself. The artist's obsession with her subjects is all that I need to drive me to work. In Artemisia Gentileschi's painting of Cleopatra, Cleopatra reclines, heavy-lidded, left hand limp on the pillow above her head. In her right hand she clutches an asp. Is this the moment before she is bitten or just after? I want to know whether, at the moment of death, that first release will stiffen. In *Danaë*, her reclining figure echoes Cleopatra's, but Danaë's left hand is limp with leisure, not surrender, while her right holds a fistful of the gold coins raining down on her naked thighs. Looking at this painting now, I don't feel leisure. I don't feel sex. I feel that I might stiffen and not be able to rise. Danaë's legs crossed at the calves and pressing against the bed cause her back to arch so that the moment of her desire mirrors Cleopatra's death. The figure retains energy, a tension that defies weariness or leisure. I like to work from the people that I see and that I want to see. What is fabric to skin, skin to violence? Sometimes

I'm concerned with using something that's in them and isn't actually visible. I try to capture the figure where the sun has darkened the skin. But that isn't the end of the neck. In *Judith Slaying Holofernes*, the light hits Judith's neck only at the base. This space between neck and breast forms a plane of skin belted with light, and I can't look away. Not the bloody knife. Not the wide eyes of Holofernes. Nothing can hold my gaze beside this neck. Artemisia has used up her patience on the neck of Judith and left nothing for the head of Holofernes. I think I use up my patience working. I use my patience looking at the skin of Judith and cannot face the dull cheek of Holofernes. Is this personal? What I increasingly feel—that awful phrase "spiritual grandeur"—I feel it like the cap of a jellyfish behind my tongue. I think a skylight must have great spiritual value. Or in Artemisia's self-portraits, what can we say about self as martyr and self as lute player? Artemisia moves her women to action and I see the painter avenging herself again and again. As I begin to make her portrait, I am conscious of the biographical. I know that I don't want the body to be read as a violated body. In each of her self-portraits, the same face swivels toward us. And as a martyr, she looks calm; as a lute-player, she suppresses a smile. Through my intimacy with the people I portray, I may have depicted aspects they find intrusive. I have worked to make her appear three-dimensional, rounded. But in this one, done by night under artificial light, the figure looks greenish, bony. A thumb peeks out from between two fingers of her left fist. She dreams. She falls backward. Cloth fills my vision. And I think I'd like to bring, out of the abyss of her figure, all the illumination of arrival. The skin is teeming. The skin has such great spirit. An entire world of light is at play just under the skin. Your calves become Danaë's calves at leisure, pressed against the grey felt in pleasure, and your bare shoulders could be Judith's shoulders, broad and reflective under skylights. But as my eyes travel up, I realize you wear the wrinkled, gutted cheek of Holofernes's half-severed head. Or you wear the same dropped countenance as the one who watches you. This image denies me body in motion, your buoyant bulk; instead, it offers a still life of skin, a cap of flesh traversed by waves of color and revealing the threshold of my own body. If I can catch a glimpse of my face reflected in the facets of the paint, in the mirror of your shoulder, I feel myself lost inside the body that I see. I see myself naked and begin to dress. What I like best is preparing for the party. I often change the fabric completely. Getting ready to go, arriving late, skipping the party, there's no difference really. It's only important to do the work. I'm doing what I want completely. This is where I lie.

Beijing

When the violence began, it was less like violence and more like parades. Students flooded the streets with bodies, horns—a hysterical mass surging forward, black and red banners pierced with holes, bodies stumbling as if hallucinating or asleep, and I want to say I am unable to write this. Or I want to say that there are two Chinas, and I can recover each with ease. I sometimes introduce myself as my child self, or to write a bio I start with my childhood. I was raised in China and sent to boarding school in Taiwan. So much about past and present is absent in this. What does China have to do with *this* portrait, *this* moment? I tell myself *stop looking*, or *look into the water, see the Medusa's self-coupling in wet concrete.* Evading house arrest, we fled, boarded a plane headed south. It was rare to travel by plane in China then, but the trains had stopped moving. Students lay across the tracks. The government ordered conductors to drive on, but the conductors said, "These are our children." I've lived alone all my life, but I never became lonely. I thought I was lucky. Things happen when you're alone. What I make myself consider before the image will appear is that there are two images. Even now, when a surgeon puts his hand through a woman's breast, or I smell the burning face peel back, reveal youth, I think of it. It's fantastic what people think they

want. I want twenty-two rooms filled with twenty-two paintings and
to run room to room, stanching the flow of paint. There's no work that
survives, and I worry that I've touched flesh, contaminated the space.
The day the secret service arrived, I had just started a home perm
and tied my head in plastic. One agent searched the apartment while
another forced me to sit on the floor. He refused to let me rinse my
hair, and it melted to brown jelly. Have I manipulated a body into the
form of the body I have known? I *will* the body solvent. And when I
look again, my appearance has changed. I have rid the curtains, the
things keeping me from seeing. I have rid the things I oppose. I hate a
homely atmosphere. I want to isolate the body away from interior and
home. Which is its knownness. Envisioning a face still young, I see
red hair splayed on the pillow, an image of a childhood that, infinite,
dissolves out of memory. Here are the plates, the etchings that happen.
I can blink my eyes, turn my head slightly, then realize I've turned
toward precise desire, a coagulation of color, of oil. The China we left
behind in Beijing is a world we could not imagine until it arrived. And
here is the China I have made into memory. Cutting, layering—all
the alterations I made to the first image flatten into a reflective plate.
An apricot chin, the shine of a jellied cheek. Flesh is so close to paint
and grafts, melts in heat. Is she a specific person? Is she related to a
specific body? We want to know. And in the photo, of course, we have
unsettled her.

IV

Eva Hesse

I have to be strict with myself. I want to say "fluency" or "ecstatic

grammars," but I try not to be swayed by fiberglass, cylindric columns

inflating and deflating, iron mesh that trails cords and petals across the

floor. Resin, vellum, wax—they are translucent, skin-like. In sunlight the

sculptures warm and glow. They take on the look of light penetrating

the thinner parts of our bodies, ears or hands. She conjures life, and it

is formal. "That's why I think I might be so good," she says. "I have no

fear. I take risks. I have the most openness about my art. My attitude

is most open. It is total freedom and the will to work." Eva Hesse had a

stepmother named Eva Hesse who had a brain tumor two years before

Eva. She got out of the hospital two years to the day Eva went in. The

same hospital and same doctor. In three years two people unrelated but

with the same name? Well, the story goes on. In this work she ties the

frame like a hospital bandage as if someone has broken an arm. A rigid

umbilical surrounds the frame. It's composed of malleable metal. Could

it expose a body? We want to know what went wrong, in the cellular, the

microscopic parts, in the lipids and tissue. *Out of domestic reflexes my

body surrounds itself.* But the body ultimately stays what it is: combines

of organ, bone, tube. It resists all sense. This first sculpture resembles

dried intestines pulled through wall. Catgut used to string instruments will last two thousand years and carry a fresher song. It's very moving, visceral of course, but restrained. As vellum's dried hide insists that there is time to consider its shape, the shape itself decays. Several of Eva's sculptures have deteriorated. They are no longer their original selves. They cannot be handled or installed as before. Consider a sculpture that, when first made, is softly draped, understated, organic, erotic, like the meninges, the protective tissue just under the skull, and is now a rigid, tawny heap. Maybe what I really want is a round table discussion about conservation. If you cut out a sizable cube of brain, it retains shape, more or less. We see the pattern develop. She only had a few hours left to live. There was so much pressure. The whole brain tipped over and all the intelligence is in the front. I'd like to try a material that will last. So many of Eva's raw materials are casting materials. But why think about them as casting materials? Imagine, instead, she makes the sculpture directly at the moment from each pliant or resistant shell. Although it's fragile, all Eva's work is tactile. The work has momentum. In *Vinculum*, everything is tenuous, knotted loosely, and can change. And I don't mind that, within reason. The work holds its tension even as the sculpture flexes, moves, and pours itself back into water. It is a life but of the most bizarre kind. Does it cry? Or grieve? Does it sting? Does it lie? Inorganic, but place your hand upon its hide and feel the waters riot, witness ecstatic grammars, fluent hands and a breaking, strong current and waves.

The Women We Were in Books

Often I see you have your hands in your pockets. Or your hands rest
on the bed and the nurse's hands rest in her pockets. The hospital
room, white linoleum day after day, your shadow blurred on the wall
behind you—how can you stand it? In this image your face shifts as
you shuttle a little emotion across its surface. As I am waiting, writing,
and from these writings making books, I am in shadow. My forehead
has passed into shadow. But the men in suits finish each hospital scene
by laughing or congratulating each other. And you say, "Why else did
God give us the bomb?" Everyone sees something changing from one
image to the next. Once, I was flattered when a teacher said to me oh
your work is so good it looks just like a man's. But, you know, I have a
real problem with women and art. "Does it label our women? Does it
ghettoize our women?" she asks. I think it is important to ask myself
why. I have assisted in many plastic surgeries. I draw inspiration from
going in to repair flesh that isn't damaged. It's a calming activity to
hold the breast and make new forms. They're crude, they're weird, but
they're wonderful to me. To look natural, the body must be somewhat
uneven. I've assisted in two kinds of plastic surgeries: additions and
subtractions. I either supplement the body so that it rounds out and
fills, or I tuck the body into itself, scraped free of excess fat. The best

part about these women is that I never know what they will become. While I watch, in my mind's eye, I also become hairdresser, stylist, and photographer. Each time something changes, the portrait changes. The knuckles of your right hand have now become the pearls of your left wrist just as my fingers fold over a cigarette. Although you don't look at your watch, the time tells us we've crossed into some other frame. What mouth you have will not release the breath. Or you hold your stomach in to trap a cough. "*Stop crying!*" I call out. I want to believe you sleep and will soon wake. That it grows light outside this room. What I see beside you is only a curtain of mist, a frame of water and breath. I'm sure of it. Sure that the lung *will fill*. I have witnessed a face relaxed and reassured myself: nothing changes. I have faced the blank page and turned it over to find your face has appeared only now. If it is not a scene at night in a lover's house but only another day in that hospital room of white linoleum, you will say, "I can still smell it," meaning decay, and press your back to the wall. Despite arthritis, despite aging, despite the overwhelming threat of decay, I recall the women we were in books. "Are you still there?" you ask. When my back is toward the camera and my heels are toward the camera, I can see the bottoms of my feet lift from the floor. What does this but memory? I retreat toward my shadow. My shadow rises to meet me, breaking the line of floor, entering the screen of the horizon. "Life is good, isn't it mama?" you will say. But could you ask me this in

Times Square? *Did you ask me this in Times Square?* I'll think. I won't remember. On the screen, you lean to the left. Your hips turn away from me. Your shoulder drops. Your head falls lower than the image of your head and your torso brightens as you pass into sun. Night approaches. Night recedes. The screen recedes. There is no explosion this time. As much as I love New York and you, we each fluctuate between being specific people, a nation, more than one nation, and an intimate void. Nothing takes the place of poetry. It fulfills a particular function. It's a mirror. I write you into the performance, and you call out. Even as I seek to bind the breast or to sculpt the face, I wonder what will happen to all these women. I'll remove what they've come to give up, I'll increase what they've come to receive, and I'll record each transaction in book and memory. But in my image of you, what I have kept or recalled looks small against your large hands; it struggles helplessly under the slight pressure of your restless thumbs.

V

Merce Cunningham

It's like night, this piece—it's like night, not moonlight but electric light, which can be turned on and off. You can turn it on and off whenever you want so that you can be in this piece and you can be in the air, which happened to me once, and the lights go out and you know the floor is there but you don't know where it is. When I first made this piece, it was about falling. Anna is high in the air, higher than most men can leap. Her right knee folds beneath her even as her left thigh, ankle, and toes extend, pressed behind into darkness. When I want to remember Anna, I know I want to remember movement. Or I want to renew sensation, to recall legs in motion, feet beating flat wood, vision and sound producing a moment transforming meaning into pure action. She comes onto the stage at a given place and performs a complicated fall to the floor, rises up, and leaves. There are no feelings in this piece—there is nothing but instinct. Anna is not just seeking the path that instinct determines. She is not attempting to bring forth the most agreeable movement. Instead, she reaches for the moment that fills the flesh in its descent, its contraction and inevitable dilation. The dancers' feet, percussion of bone on wood, a sound simultaneously hollow and dense, heard yet felt. Almost anything you look at you can see in terms of movement, but on the blackened stage our limbs become estranged, become phantom limbs for moments at a time. You feel the imagined borders, the broken tones that compose the flesh, dissolve. And, really, this is how you come to know that your own body is a phantom. Like a skier or a football player, I put black paint under my eyes. Smudging the black thrills me. I become somebody else out in the dark, even as the piece refuses to tell me what to look at or to listen to—what body I now possess. I've never had arms. All I've ever had are stumps. Yet I've always experienced phantom limbs. I continually attempt to gesture, gesticulate, reach out, grasp, grab, point, wave, shake hands, or motion for the check. Movement does not explain sensation. My limbs have always known what Anna's limbs reveal: beyond standing up, there is sitting down, and beyond sitting down, there is lying down, and, beyond this, one falls. In my vision of dance, the large feet of the figures often do not lend themselves to walking. I prefer having the possibilities that a woman gives in movement. Women have a continuous quality, which can go on really for quite some time. I very much wanted to make something for the dancers which had fluidity, airy, light, something less rooted or anchored to the ground so that, by the fifth panel, Anna is almost transparent and has left the picture plane. In *Summerspace*, she becomes all turns. That's one of her secrets. She is standing there with energy coming up and out her sternum. Her energy originates in the solar plexus. As she moves, her sternum pulls her across the stage.

Is this why you walk so beautifully, I ask. Yes. The figure walks as if pulled by a string. This is why Anna is most ready to change direction. She steps forward, lands on the ball of her foot. The purest expression of meaning in movement is that, although we all walk using the same mechanism and patterns, we all walk differently. We become ourselves in our walk as well as in our speech. We don't have to give the walk a meaning to convince someone. We just walk. It is the dancer being herself completely, not in a mannered step, but in a full step that then makes the step independently alive. And the dancers, rather than being someone, do something. In using the ground for support, in walking along stage or street, we pull these surfaces into our bodies. The stage is alive in the moment we have involved it in our own functions, extended the limb into the asphalt and called the asphalt to service. And I cannot help but ask, if the brain region responsible for smooth swinging of the arms differs from the one that controls gesturing, are my gestures then Anna's grace? I do see these different bodies in my work as connected. A leg is the size of an observed leg; a foot is someone's real foot. But rather than rendering such shapes life-like, they become outlines, the bare minimum of detail, just pointers—a white feather horizontal or a white hip laid down. The torso is a pink soundstage, a movement between a dinner plate and the mouth. Or between paradise and the lyric, leading down. Our whole body sees itself in the raw linen of the legs. We make a record of our movement, our work together—such a wide territory and subject to all types of conditions like humidity, light, heat. In *Beach Birds for the Camera*, she yields to temptation, to the rhythm of armature and body mass, so that every large female back as variation runs through our image just as it runs through a piece of music. *Diastole-systole: the world that seizes you by closing in around you, the self that opens to the world, opens the world itself.* We can't move in the way animals move. We can't pretend to imitate this. In this piece, each dancer wears white tights, white torso interrupted by a black band at the chest covering the shoulders, arms, hands. The striking lines of the costumes suggest a colony of water birds. The soft focus, limpid light, grainy black and white cinematography evoke weather and air. The pads of the feet hit the stage in fits and thuds as Anna spreads her slender arms over you, brushing your bowed head with her face. All these feet, ankles, knees, and toes, seeing them together like this, as a crowd… I spend all my time in the studio now, alone. I touch her cheek. What do you feel? You are touching my cheek. Anything else? You are touching my lips. Are you sure? Yes. I can feel it both places. You are rubbing my forearms. The lung. The wing. Anna abandons her head to the camera. She sees herself in a head that belongs to the camera, that has disappeared into the camera.

Shenzhen II

Chu Yun's early portrait of the city, *Who Has Stolen Our Bodies*, shows
twenty-seven bars of used soap gathered from friends and arrayed
atop a white plinth. Each pastel-colored bar has been worn down,
diminished, and abandoned after use. Now anti-monuments, they are
non-objects that exist only because someone has decided to stop using
them. They recall the contours of the absent bodies. The rounded
corners reproduce the negative space of arm's pocket, hip's ridge,
hollow of the eye socket, lips' indent, wrinkles of the face. These stiff
figures of memory remain as estranged forms, as refugees. Looking
at the reflection of my face in the white shine of the plinth, I think
how much tidier to have been born old and aged into a child, brought
finally to the brink, not of the grave, but of home. I've heard there are
beautiful beaches here, maybe as close as an hour away, but I've never
seen them. The stretches of sand closer in are littered with rubber
tubing, syringes, empty pill bottles. I collect it all in a metal box and
bury it as treasure. The beach stinks and rots around me. Eroded rocks
crumble out in the bay, resembling crusted lace or moth-eaten linen.
Covered in birds and completely white with bird shit, these rocks rise
near-celestial against the soot-filled sky. Shenzhen is neither a tourist
destination nor home. Each resident has immigrated from somewhere

else. Each body displaced and dispersed among the stiff architecture of apartment buildings. *In China, the human body has never been seen to have its own intrinsic glory.* I lived here for years among the currents of mobile labor and outsourced production that define the Pearl River Delta. I've tried to untangle myself from Shenzhen's webs of commerce and daily life, humidity, stench, pollution, traffic, construction, and manic border zones. Yet, in *Constellation*, Chu Yun's rendering of his cramped Shenzhen apartment still alludes to my present body. The physical self has been loosely arranged as used electronics: a water cooler, printer, or TV. What vision of Shenzhen is recalled by so many flashing lights? Go back into yourself and look, Chu Yun would say. If you do not yet see yourself beautiful, then cut away, polish. I walk into a dark room. As my eyes adjust to darkness, I become aware that flashing lights emanate from electrical appliances. They are either in *Pause* or *Error* mode. I ask him, "Why all this barbarity?" He answers that he loves beauty and would have it about him. In my memory of the city, I discover a woman who is a beast turning human. Or if you're drawn toward cities with a lather of misery, if you want to find a population that will be locked together in the end, then you are on the trail toward our port of poor beasts. You are approaching our mildewed harbor invaded by figures of mangrove and steel scaffolding that have twined their antlers and are found dead that way, their heads fattened with a knowledge of one another they

never wanted, having to contemplate each other head-on until death.
What an autopsy I could make of Shenzhen with everything askew in
her bowels! A kidney and a shoe cast of Imperial Beijing; a liver and
a long-spent whisper of Sichuan; a gall and a wrack of scolds from
Gansu; the lining of her belly flocked with the locks cut off love in
Shanghai and her people coming down the grim path of "We know
not" to "We can't guess." To be a body in this city is to rob yourself
for everyone, to become incapable of giving yourself warning; it is to
be continually turning about to find yourself diminished. I'd like to
shoot a clean image without mentioning aspects such as the place's
historic stature, victory spot of the revolution, the Red cradle, and so
on. I'd like the image to show this city as a beautiful place. Instead, the
image reveals the way the body escapes from itself through the delta's
open mouth, the anus or stomach of the bay, through the circle of the
plastic washbasin in each kitchen, the point of an umbrella at each
door. In Shenzhen I have known the soul is figure and form, a frothing
of blood around the heart. The soul is a substance. Chu Yun decorates
our city with brightly-colored flags of announcement. From the top of
each gray tower he hangs lines of pink, red, gold, and blue triangles,
crisscrossing the scaffolding, forming a bright grid upon the yellow
cranes and the green fruit trees. The flags insist the body should shine
with happiness, with banal beauty and feigned promise. The flags insist
that there is laughter, incorporated into the city and tinged with the

smoke and noise of our streets. Chu Yun succeeds in finding the stag beetle to be something hard and fierce and intestinal worms to contain a determined countenance. As to our costal plants, what an expression of love in the lychee trees! Eight thousand snapshots of his own tiny apartment, glued in thick stacks so that only the top image is seen, his physiognomy of our living bodies. A mesh of markings, organic labyrinth of meanings, Shenzhen offers us her great cosmogonies of thought, human faces, bodies. Outside, small brown lizards cover the courtyard. Children break off the tails to lay them in rows.

VI

Illness, the Flash at the Lens

I generally know I am sick the moment I take the photo. I build a
certain tension. For example, I cannot work if you are there behind
me, listening to music. We need to be completely concentrated, still.
Then I begin to sense the start of the illness, the tiny flash against the
lens. There are times I begin to obsess about illness and instead I hear
her voice on the radio: *We owe we owe we do not exist at least not*
collectively. But that really depends on the day. Some days the prints
emerge as happy mistakes. It really is accidental—I spill the wrong
chemical on the press, she adds a line or two concerning degeneration,
the chemical eats through page after page, and presto. I try not to put
anyone in a box, she says. Because they want complete control. Or
I say I'm sorry to someone but god knows who. And in a now-I'm-
telling-you-this voice I was going to say, well, the one thing I can say
is that I'm not interested in giving you an American poem. Are you
thinking like an actress when you are being filmed? she asks. Is she
thinking like an actress when she's being stuck over and over with the
same damn needle? She enters her own fantastic world, that extremely
square waiting room, its pink plastic upholstery all pointing to this
next photo or diagnosis. When you make a diagnosis, there's no
fiction. Once, at St. Luke's, the king of the Roma needed heart surgery.

This was before I worked there but it had become legend or people still imagined the king to be a character in our hospital drama. If you were there, you saw yourself as a distraught woman dreaming of some other life. The room became the king's private waiting room. The pink waiting room will hold you in a vision of real luxury: Hotel de Crillon, bare legs, body reclining on a bed. It does tell a story and then to haul that story out of the building with you when you've been discharged— well, let's try it. In the face, there is a certain harshness combined with something more theatrical. I'm sure that I express a fantasy different from my own. Which, to an extent, is Paris. And I have to ask why is it that we've worked together twice and both times at the Crillon? I found the architecture overwhelming. Later, in that basement bar, the stone, the five-hundred-year-old arches, it all felt like bringing the metaphor to life—hitting rock bottom, and the bottom is a wine cellar that serves great fries. That's the problem with Paris as a setting. You're not defined by weather or the people watching you. Things happen like invention, invasion, more and better kinds of intrusion. The bare legs are just substitution for the wrist that bends and will not break, the impenetrable utensil we *wish* we were presenting to the nurse, we wish we were moving across the page, marking, scraping, scrimshawing *other people's vision*. If you hear about great directors, they all work like that. You have to push these accidents to happen. At the same time, you have to be in control. In hospitals, people are always concerned

with what the neighbors will say. At St. Luke's many older nurses
wore dresses and stood when the surgeons entered the room. In your
vision of Paris, they became wilder. Our grandmothers became rogue
aunts, always wearing their white nurses' caps. Which is the humor of
the work. It's a space where you're left alone. How can we dis-attach
ourselves? There she was on the bed in the Crillon, fingers laced on
the pillow, hip digging into the mattress. She had all her makeup on,
but maybe she'd been crying. Her mouth and nose seemed abnormally
pink. And all these freckles coating her bare arms. She's not young. *All
my life, since I was ten, I've wanted to be in this hell here with you. All
I've ever wanted and still I do.* There's a word for skin, not epidermis
and closer to epithalamus but less to do with the brain than everything
else about the body. With my portraits, when I am in front of the
camera, I have a good sense of the camera. I have an incredible sense
of the vessel's spectrum, the lens and where the needle should be. If
I can't control all these parameters, then I have to recreate the whole
thing again. This happens quite often. I reshoot until I have exactly
what I want. During the shoot, the nurse is present in a way that puts
me at ease. This allows us to go further. That was the hell poem and
right now she reads an anyone poem. In one more poem she'll read the
heaven poem. There is such great presence. They're very carnal. There
is so much skin. This is the poem. Eventually, we want to fill the vial.

The Photo Does Not Exhaust Itself

This photo is about family. In the photo, he's sixteen. His horse stands with loose reins beside an alpine lake. The water looks less like water than sky, and even in the heat of August my father rests just below the snow line. Although it's not polite to speak about family, I don't mind. I go ahead and pick up what's around. There's a moment just before embarking on a portrait when there's just enough time to make a quick prayer. I am desperate to feel the elation of the image—I want to know the moment I've begun. The event shown in the image I am making of my father—the event or theme, I don't know what to call it—is an instant in a cemetery. You stop in front of a flooded hole and gaze in. You see the bottom of an alpine lake. You see the instant of that fantasy or you see the instant of what might be memory, which, in another instant, will be gone. No one wants me to mention my father's youngest brother. He was a lonely child. Playing in the barn, he hung himself. I think he was playing out the hanging scenes in old westerns. Before my grandfather died, he showed me a wooden box shaped like a pyramid. It had belonged to my uncle and held toy horses. As I reached for the plastic horses, my grandfather started to cry, whispering, "It was very sad when Scott was young and caught an illness in his throat." I don't want to make a clear image. I spend enormous amounts of time looking for photos with just the right

amount of decrepitude. The phantasm of the rainy cemetery recurs.

It gives rise to an image I thought might be good—a memory that

must be something more than its subject, that must permit me to see

more than what is there. I have already seen something like it before.

The earth doesn't care where a death occurs. Its job is to efface and

renew. The land isn't going to remember by itself, but the image will.

This photo has the right feeling. There are upright stones and old

statues. It has the solitary, well-placed trees that we might identify

with cemeteries. All the shooting is strictly documentary, very straight

photography. It's the process that Brady used in the civil war and

Fenton and Gardner used out west with their mule teams. You have

to wait for the right light, and you capture what is there. I don't know

if it is even possible to make an image of this kind of family tragedy. I

know it is not possible to allow myself to name those who have died

in the photo. Photography wants to prove there is only one world, not

many—one visible world. But that is only a plea made by photography,

not a conclusion. These pale, nearly white images, an abandoned wall

or a fallen tree, evoke loss. My father pastes new paper to the walls

in the cabin and re-planks the porch, which offers a view across the

meadows to the peaks. I am left struggling with my fragile perception,

filling in the gaps with imagined scenarios. The photo admits the

light leaks and flaws of process. These distortions, these blotches or scratches, they matter. I learned from a doctor that collodion, a chemical essential to my work, was used for surgery in the Civil War to bind wounds. I set the lenses on the lake's edge. Next, I acquire material from the lake floor. I want to take a snapshot of the lake floor. I include only what might have really been seen there at a given instance. I would dredge a living moment from the water.

Helen

Helen is of course that Helen of Sparta. Helen of Troy. Helena hated of
Greece. In a dream or trance she left Troy. She finds herself in Egypt.
You must be patient, remembering. You can choose where. We are
going to see whatever we haven't seen and maybe that means traveling
down instead of across. Some say Taiwan gets better surf than China's
southern beaches because it is out in the Pacific Ocean and exposed
to larger swells. We camped at Bai Xia Wan. Soon Helen's skin peeled
off in one snaking tube, leaving behind pink stinging surface. I lived in
the south and there were always rich oil kids around. One of the great
things about Taiwan, something not really true of China, is that there
are a lot of small beaches where you can surf on your own. You have
to watch the weather. Once, at Bai Xia, I tried to save a surfer who was
drowning. I tried desperately to save him for almost twenty minutes
but he didn't make it. Paradise, that idea of being together, of fusion
or whatever it might look like. *Here there is peace. For Helena. Helena*
hated of all Greeks. For Helen, the ocean is a way to talk about raw
force. Of course, the deep sea is unknown. "More people have traveled
into space than have gone down to those abyssal depths," she says. This
work is work I made as we tread. While out on the coast, I kept cutting
into the work, drawing over it. After living overseas for more than a

decade, I had been altered in the way I had to be altered in order to enter a new lexicon, to become at once a "one" and "not one" of local culture. Whatever happened to me, I never felt out of place, like I shouldn't be here, in this vertigo of inducing. A female traveler is a jewel-encrusted fan: Helen. She's standing on the beach but the beach has turned to scrub brush or the tide is just out and silver is beneath the water. She sheds a silver snakeskin, broken speech. We see life and call it beauty. It is magnificent, wonderful. Remembering this scene, I see fever in her face. The sheen is so plasticine it recalls salt-eaters, *salmon en croute*, inky saturation, smudges, staining. It retells our whole history, a record of perforations, *la parlourde, la morue, coquille St. Jacque, le filet de plié*, and each notation we put in place so that we remember. Who are we? Who directs us? And after traveling so long together? Yes, it's this voluminous nothing that at the time is very real but later, trying to hold it still for a moment, it's then that we have reached for, or that we are straining toward, some first sight of home.

NOTES

The book's epigraph is taken from a Jean-Luc Nancy essay titled "Imm-Trans." *Polygraph* 15/16 (2004): 11-12.

"Still Life with Rayfish" contains a quote from the film *Jacob's Ladder*, directed by Adrian Lyne (1990). Italicized text is excerpted from *The Secret Books of the Egyptian Gnostics* by Jean Doresse (Inner Traditions International, 1986). "Once I saw the village butcher [...] I still have not succeeded" is a remark Soutine made to his friend and biographer, Emil Szittya, recorded in *Soutine et son temps* (La Bibliothèque des Arts, Paris, 1955), and quoted in *Chaim Soutine, Catalogue Raisonné*, eds. Maurice Tuchman, Esti Dunow, Klaus Perls, Benedikt Taschen Verlag (Köln, Taschen, 2001).

"Andy Warhol" incorporates and adapts quotations from Warhol's conversations in *The Philosophy of Andy Warhol: from A to B and back again*, Andy Warhol (Harcourt Books, 1975).

"Total Hip Replacement" incorporates and adapts comments from an interview between Jenny Saville and Simon Schama in *Jenny Saville* (Rizzoli, 2005). Italicized text is excerpted from Gertrude Stein's essay "Composition as Explanation," first published in *What Are Masterpieces?* (Hogarth Press, 1926).

"Everything Is Autobiography and Everything Is a Portrait" adapts comments from a conversation between Lucian Freud and William Feaver in *Lucian Freud* (Rizzoli, 2007).

"Eva Hesse" incorporates and adapts comments from an interview with Hesse in *ART TALK: Conversations with 15 Women Artists*, by Cindy Nemser (Harper Collins, 1975). Italicized text is excerpted from *War Variations* by Amelia Rosselli, translated by Lucia Re and Paul Vangelisti (Green Integer, 2005).

"The Women We Were in Books" incorporates and adapts comments from an interview with Ida Applebroog on *Art 21*, Season 3, *Power: Ida Applebroog* (2005) and considers images from Applebroog's 1981 artist's books *A Performance, Stop Crying, So?, It's Very Simple, Mean It*, and *Can't*.

"Merce Cunningham": italicized text is adapted from *Francis Bacon: The Logic of Sensation* by Gilles Deleuze, translated by Daniel W. Smith (University of Minnesota Press, 2005).

"Shenzhen II" adapts phrases from *Nightwood* by Djuana Barnes (New Directions, 1937). Italicized text is from "Tales of *Shen* and *Xin*: Body Person and Heart-Mind in China during the Last 150 Years" by Mark Elvin in *Zone 4: Fragments for a History of the Human Body: Part Two* (MIT, 1989).

"Illness, the Flash at the Lens" adapts comments from Jeurgen Teller's interview with Marie Darrieussecq in *Juergen Teller: Do You Know What I Mean* (Thames & Hudson, 2006). It also adapts comments and quotes the italicized poem fragment from Alice Notley's reading at Kelly Writers House, November 6, 2006, available on Penn Sound http://writing.upenn.edu/pennsound/x/Notley.php.

"The Photo Does Not Exhaust Itself" incorporates and adapts comments from an interview with Sally Mann in the film *What Remains: The Life and Work of Sally Mann* (2006).

"Helen": The Portuguese sailors who stumbled upon Taiwan in 1547 named it Ilha Formosa, meaning Beautiful Island. Italicized text is from H.D.'s *Helen in Egypt* (New Directions, 1974).

ACKNOWLEDGMENTS

Many thanks to the editors of *Clock, Fourteen Hills, jubilat, OmniVerse,* and *Phantom Limb* for publishing work from this collection.

Thank you Robyn Schiff and *Boston Review* for featuring "Still Life with Rayfish," "Merce Cunningham," and "Shenzhen" in the Poet's Sampler. Thank you Shane McCrae and PEN USA for featuring "If the Heart Does Not Restart," "The Photo Does Not Exhaust Itself," and "The Women We Were in Books" in the PEN Poetry Series.

I am grateful to the Iowa Arts Council and the Lincoln Arts Council for grants that aided in the completion of these poems.

Special thanks to Rusty Morrison, Ken Keegan, Gillian Hamel, and Cassandra Smith for their support of this work. And to Caryl Pagel and Lynn Xu for believing in this book from the start.

Mary Hickman was born in Idaho and grew up in China and Taiwan. She is the author of the poetry collection *This Is the Homeland*. She is a visiting professor at Nebraska Wesleyan University, and teaches in the University of Iowa International Writing Program's Between the Lines exchange program.

Rayfish
by Mary Hickman

Cover art by Robert Fernandez
Rayfish, mixed media, 2016

Cover and interior typefaces: Minion Pro

Interior design by Cassandra Smith

Offset printed in the United States
by Edwards Brothers Malloy, Ann Arbor, Michigan
On 55# Glatfelter B18 Antique
Acid Free Archival Quality Recycled Paper

Publication of this book was made possible in part by gifts from:
The New Place Fund
Robin & Curt Caton

Omnidawn Publishing
Oakland, California
2017

Rusty Morrison & Ken Keegan, senior editors & co-publishers
Gillian Olivia Blythe Hamel, managing editor
Cassandra Smith, poetry editor & book designer
Sharon Zetter, poetry editor, book designer & development officer
Liza Flum, poetry editor & marketing assistant
Peter Burghardt, poetry editor
Juliana Paslay, fiction editor
Gail Aronson, fiction editor
Cameron Stuart, marketing assistant
Avren Keating, administrative assistant
Kevin Peters, *OmniVerse* Lit Scene editor
Sara Burant, *OmniVerse* reviews editor
Josie Gallup, publicity assistant
SD Sumner, copyeditor
Briana Swain, marketing assistant